DROPSHIPPING BUSINESS STRATEGY

STEP BY STEP 1 HOUR BEGINNER'S GUIDE TO MAKING MONEY ONLINE

Table Of Contents

INTRODUCTION 4
   Why drop shipping?..4
   Platforms to drop ship...6
   Why Amazon?..6
   Why Amazon FBA?..7
CHAPTER 1 8
THE BEST WAYS TO PICK A PROFITABLE PRODUCT TO SELL 8
CHAPTER 2 15
HOW TO EFFECTIVELY WORK WITH OVERSEAS SUPPLIERS 15
CHAPTER 3 27
HOW TO BRAND YOUR FBA BUSINESS 27
CHAPTER 4 30
HOW TO SET UP YOUR AMAZON SELLER ACCOUNT 30
   How to calculate your profit margins..32
   How feedback relates to sales..34
CHAPTER 5 44
HOW TO AUTOMATE YOUR DROP SHIPPING ORDERS 44
CHAPTER 6 47
THE TOP 5 BEST SELLING NICHES 47
   5. Sporting Goods...47
   4. Hardware and tools 48
   3. Organizational products..48
   2. Creative storage 49
   1. Alternative energy based products 50
CONCLUSION..54

Copyright 2017 by Bookitover - All rights reserved.

This document is geared towards providing exact and reliable information in regards to the topic and issue covered. The publication is sold with the idea that the publisher is not required to render accounting, officially permitted, or otherwise, qualified services. If advice is necessary, legal or professional, a practiced individual in the profession should be ordered. From a Declaration of Principles which was accepted and approved equally by a Committee of the American Bar Association and a Committee of Publishers and Associations. In no way is it legal to reproduce, duplicate, or transmit any part of this document in either electronic means or in printed format. Recording of this publication is strictly prohibited and any storage of this document is not allowed unless with written permission from the publisher. All rights reserved. The information provided herein is stated to be truthful and consistent, in that any liability, in terms of inattention or otherwise, by any usage or abuse of any policies, processes, or directions contained within is the solitary and utter responsibility of the recipient reader. Under no circumstances will any legal responsibility or blame be held against the publisher for any reparation, damages, or monetary loss due to the information herein, either directly or indirectly. Respective authors own all copyrights not held by the publisher. The information herein is offered for informational purposes solely, and is universal as so. The presentation of the information is without contract or any type of guarantee assurance. The trademarks that are used are without any consent, and the publication of the trademark is without permission or backing by the trademark owner. All trademarks and brands within this book are for clarifying purposes only and are the owned by the owners themselves, not affiliated with this document.

INTRODUCTION

Do you ever wake up to this in your email box: Make millions of dollars through drop shipping! Make $150,000 from home in the next 90 days by drop shipping! How about making millions just working for 1 hour in a day? It sounds too good to be true right? However, do you know that this is actually very true? You can actually become financially free working for just a few hours in a day. I used to be a doubting Thomas like you too until I discovered the drop shipping path to make millions.

Why drop shipping?

Drop shipping is highly recommended for five main reasons:

1. It is a low-risk business (imagine not risking to buy an inventory that will not sell). You only need to purchase a product when you have an existing order to fulfill. Also, you aren't stuck with thousands of products that you have to sell at a loss if things don't work out.

2. It is a very easy way to sell physical products online.

3. You can offer a larger number of products to your customer since you don't have to pre-purchase all the items that you sell at once.

4. You can decide to run your drop shipping business from anywhere with a laptop and an internet connection because you won't have to worry about fulfillment or running a warehouse.

5. It is relatively easy to scale since you don't need to fulfill each order manually

With that said, **what exactly is drop shipping?**

It is a supply chain management technique whereby the retailer does not have to keep goods in stock. Rather, transfers his customers' orders and shipment details to either a manufacturer or a wholesaler who are responsible for shipping the goods directly to the customer.

Retailers make profit by

- The difference between the wholesale and the retail price or,

- An agreed percentage of the sales in commission. This is paid by the wholesaler.

Platforms to drop ship

This is the first headache of any drop shipper;

"How do I market my products?" The three most common ways of marketing your drop ship products are:

- Listing on eBay
- Listing on craigslist
- Listing on Amazon

However, in this guide, we will be focusing on selling your drop ship products through Amazon. We will refer to this as fulfillment by Amazon (or Amazon FBA for short).

Why Amazon?

One major reason: Amazon is unarguably the number one e-commerce retailer in the world. (Yes, you are permitted to use Google to confirm this).

When you list your products on Amazon, it gets seen by thousands of customers each day.

More specifically now,

Why Amazon FBA?

As a seller, you can leverage on Amazon's credibility to:

- Expand and efficiently distribute your goods
- Provide awesome customer service for your orders

In this guide, you will discover...

- The best ways to pick a profitable product to sell
- How to effectively work with overseas suppliers
- How to brand your FBA business
- How to set up your Amazon seller account
- How you can use feedback to grow your sales
- How to automate your drop shipping orders
- The top 5 best-selling niches

CHAPTER 1

THE BEST WAYS TO PICK A PROFITABLE PRODUCT TO SELL

In this chapter, you will discover

- The exact criteria you need to know when you're trying to locate winning products.

- The three-step process to find products that have high buyer demand but low seller competition

- How to research items that have the potential to be profitable.

To do this, we're going to find products that meet the following criteria;

- 50 reviews or less - they are selling at least 3000 units or more a month

- Their selling price is less than $50 and

- Weigh 2 to 3 pounds or less.

You see our goal is to find an item where the sellers are selling lots of units a month despite having low numbers of reviews. If we can find a great item that has lots of sales despite low numbers of reviews, then we know that it will not be difficult for us to come and replicate our competition and then beat them.

Since this guide is for beginners, I don't want you to choose products that are difficult to manufacture and ship, that's why I set the price to be a maximum of $50. Usually, if an item costs $20 or more, it becomes more expensive to manufacture and ship it. We don't want our products to weigh more than two pounds, because that will make shipping expensive which will reduce our profit margins.

However, to find these Unicorn products can be very tasking. Do you know that Amazon has more than million items in its online catalog? Thus, there are millions of products on the website. So, it can make the product research seem very difficult. I mean where are you going to start?

Here is a manual method:

Amazon helps us here by literally telling you the best selling products. Simply go to Amazon, click on any category, then click the best sellers link and you'll see the best selling products for that category listed in order of which is selling the most and making the most amount of money.

Just type the link on the screen to go directly to a list of all the best-selling products in every single category. Want an even quicker way? We're going to be using a tool that will do the hard work for us - The product database tools by the jungle scout team.

This tool is going to save us days if not weeks of research time to use this tool you will need access to their web app subscription. Now you only need to use the lowest cost subscription the start-up addition to access the product database tool.

Here's a link to a video that shows you how to use the jungle scout app:

\>> htttps://www.youtube.com/watch?v=LRhJWNah9Ys

Pro tip: Change the criteria settings to show results to the 200th page rather than the default so just come and select Use the tracker tool that comes with the jungle scout app to filter your results. Search the results and look for items that meet the following criteria;

- They are not a big brand product
- They are not bulky
- They are not difficult to manufacture and not likely to break easily on transit and
- They don't require us to create variations now.

Obviously, we want to avoid competing with big brand products because they will be very difficult to compete with. Plus, we want to avoid big bulky items because they will be expensive to ship. We should also filter out items that look like they will be difficult to manufacture or delicate items that can break in transit, because that will reduce our profit margin.

So items that include little electronics are the sorts of things that we want to avoid now. Once you have successfully manufactured and private labeled your first products, you may want to move on to items that are more challenging.

To order your first item, I recommend that you keep things simple which is also why we don't want to have to worry about items that would require us to manufacture multiple variations of such as clothing. This kind of product would require us to create different sizes because this is basically like creating multiple products and now we have to manage more inventory, and we just don't want to have to deal with that now.

When most people try to find items to manufacture/sell, they usually make some mistakes-

1. They think of the items that people use all the time. For example, Pins Pierce would be a great product, but you'll have stiff competitions from established sellers if you try to sell the products.
2. The second mistake that people make is that they only want to sell items that are related to hobbies

or interests. They'll say, I love coffee, so, I'll sell coffee accessories. Board games? I'm going to manufacture and sell board game accessories now.

Don't get me wrong it's a nice bonus if you get to sell an item that interests you, but do not get stuck in the mentality of only selling items that interest you. When analyzing our market competition and our market dips we want to find items where we can compete with the price point of at least $20 because this will give us a healthy profit after FBA Costs and of course manufacturing cost.

Bonus step: analyze the SEO competition for an item. When you manufacture an item for Amazon, your goal is to come in and steal the sales away from your competitors. One way to do this is to manufacture a product that is better than your competitors, ' and I do recommend that everybody does this. The other way is to get more views than them and get a higher review score. You're not going to be able to do this in the beginning, but you should be working your way towards this. But another thing that you can do right from the very start is to make a better listing than your competitors.

When I say make a better listing, I mean make a listing that converts better than your competitors and is also better optimized for the internal Amazon search engine. If you can locate an item that has high buyer demand, low seller competition and also lower SEO competition, then you're in a great position to come and manufacture your products. Before this bonus step, you will need either a standard or business subscription to the jungle Scout web app.

CHAPTER 2

HOW TO EFFECTIVELY WORK WITH OVERSEAS SUPPLIERS

By overseas suppliers, I mean manufacturers, who make/build the product that you want to sell on Amazon. The reason is that if you go and find a product that's used or even new, being sold at a yard sale or Craigslist, then you turn around and sell it for a profit, that's good. The problem is you make that money one time. And then you have to repeat the process all over again, and it's really hard to become financially independent this way.

The importance of finding a supplier/manufacturer is that you can buy one product that you know better. Then you know you can get ten, twenty, a hundred, a thousand duplicates of that same product and when you sell it on Amazon. It keeps making you money, and you've only have post it once, and you just keep selling it over and over again.

In this chapter, we will discuss the two proven places you can go to find a supplier. You're also going to discover how to watch out for scammers. So here we go: Let's say you found a product on Amazon that you're convinced is going to be marketable, then you're going to head over to Alibaba.com.

Let's say the product is a USB cable; you hit the search bar and then all these USB cable products on Alibaba will pop up. Now the first thing you want to do is find a supplier that you can trust, and the easiest way to do that is you look at the information beside the seller's name.

- The little gold star or circle means a gold supplier;
- The 1-yr (one year) it means they have only been a supplier for one year.

Pro tip: Only go with suppliers who are two-years gold suppliers or more.

For a supplier to be a gold supplier on Alibaba, the administration at Alibaba physically visited that suppliers' factory and gave them the approval certificate that they are verified and trusted. They looked at their company, their financials, their employees, their employers and their products.

Though some suppliers have been able to get under the radar and pretend to be gold suppliers, but later it turns out they were just renting the factory or doing something else. Therefore, be careful about going even with a one year supplier. When you go for suppliers with two or more years of sales, the chances are slim that they would scam you. I've never been scammed since I adopted this strategy of going with a two-year supplier or more.

Note- Every other thing on their product description page matters too.

For example, what's their minimum order of quantity? A one piece minimum order is good. That means you can order just one sample, send it in Amazon FBA and see how it does. This is to test the product before making a major financial commitment.

How many inquiries have they had in the last 90 days? Above 300 is good enough.

How many numbers of views have they had within the same period? 2,000+ views are ideal enough.

What is their payment term?

What methods of payment are they willing to accept from you the buyer? Do they accept LC, TT, western union or money gram?

Do they want a hundred percent payment in advance?

Pro tip: Never go with Western Union or TT.

Reason: Experienced sellers say there's no way to hold the supplier accountable if the product never comes through. Once you make payment through Western Union, it will go straight to the supplier and there's no way to get it back if there is any issue.

What I recommend is PayPal payment. That way, if they tried to cheat, you could go in and dispute it. PayPal will put that money on hold, and you can prove they never ship this item. The suppliers would have to show a tracking number to verify they shipped the products to you and if they can't do that, then you will get your money back.

Secondly, you could also go with Trade assurance. Trade Assurance means you can place your order online using your credit card and that money goes into a third party holding company, like an escrow, and you only pay part of it upfront.

They build a product then you pay the rest, and they ship it out. They don't get their money until you verify that you've received and you're satisfied with the product, and so it's almost impossible for them to scam you. PayPal and Trade Assurance are two reliable ways to protect yourself from being scammed. Once you decide this is a product you want to try to sell, just click on "contact supplier". Now that you are here, you want to type in a message, and I've learned the hard way what to type in and what not to.

Keep it super simple. Since they are in China, there's going to likely be a language barrier. So use simple words.

Ask everything you need up front to save you time. Typically when it's 2 p.m in Austin Texas: it's 2 a.m. or a little later over there. So there's a 12-hour difference in that time zone. Basically, it's going to take a while to get the information back, so you're not going to get a response till the next day. Unless you want to work deep into the night, and this is not recommended.

Sample questions you can ask the suppliers

- **What is the cost if you order just one sample?**

This is important because if you order for one sample, you can test it before committing to a large shipment.

If one sample is not allowed, then, what is the minimum order that they can allow you to order right away? Most companies will not let you buy one. They're going to require you to buy a hundred or 1000. In most cases, they're going to say you have to order at least 100 before they will create bundles of the product for you.

Occasionally, you can have a company that will allow you to order for one piece.

If you order just one at the cost of $30, then, add another $20 for shipping. So, it's going to be like paying $50 or $60 for a test sample. This may seem crazy for just one little product, but remember you're doing it so you can test it if that product sells within a week on Amazon FBA or within a seven-day period.

I can guarantee you that if this product is going to sell; it's worth spending that time. Once you have done that and it proves to sell very well and to your satisfaction, then you can order a whole lot more based on how much capital you have. Then, send all of your orders to Amazon, and that's where you start selling and making a lot of money.

Notice also, the shipping costs by express air (airplane) or sea. Now if it's a sample, shipping by air is highly recommended. Let's say you like what you hear then the next message you're going to send is "please send me API." The API is also known as a pro-forma invoice.

Usually, it'll be in an excel spreadsheet. It's going to show you a picture of the product, how many units, the total cost for products and the shipping costs. If it's through PayPal, Paypal fees will also be included.

Pro tip: Once you develop a close relationship with a supplier if they always take orders through PayPal you can ask them: "May I send you the money as Friend and Family option instead of using the service payment option?" What that does is to remove the fees because otherwise, you will always have to pay for those fees as a buyer. This will save you a lot of money especially if your order is more than $10,000.

This option will save you a ton of money when you negotiate with suppliers. Always ask for a better deal and when you're negotiating with the supplier;

This tip always work effectively

"Look, I'm a new company, and I just started out. If I like this product, I'd be interested in a long term relationship with you. Would you be willing to come down three cents or ten or fifteen cents on each product?"

That may not seem like a lot of money, but when the day comes, and you're ordering 500- 20000 piece of these products, you will be saving yourself a lot of money, and your profit margins will increase even if it is just a dollar off. Most of the time, the supplier will be happy to reduce the price for you, and you just saved yourself money just because you asked.

They're used to that; they're just used to negotiating because it is a free market and you're sending them your money and trusting them to send you the product.

Some people have this fear of purchasing from China. But if you don't realize it, most of the products that we use every day are actually manufactured in China. The quality of the product is more important than the country where the product is being manufactured. This is the second reason a sample should be ordered first. If you get the sample, you can test it. For example, if it's a track pad, you can get a hammer and hit it.

In fact, you might want to order two or three samples so you can break one and test out the others on Amazon. You can test it, squeeze it, and bit it. Your mission is to know if this Singapore-made product is worth turning in as a product to be sold for a long period of time.

I always recommend you get a sample first to not only test it yourself but also to test it in the marketplace. Once you are satisfied with the test samples, you have agreed to the terms, and you have made the payment, be patient.

Some companies may have thousands of units in their store that they can ship to you right away, while some other companies will have to go and manufacture it from their factory. This alone can take two to three weeks. Thus it's important that you develop other different streams of income. Don't just focus on one thing and be willing to be patient; it will pay off. After shipment, it may take less than a week if it's shipped by air. For sea shipping, it is often a week and a half to three weeks long.

An Alternate option to Alibaba: Dhgate.

Dhgate is a completely different animal. Dhgate is smaller compared with Alibaba, but Alibaba has a higher number of scammers than Dhgate. Dhgate has much more strict rules, so it's much less likely that you're going to get scammed.

In general, Alibaba can get you a larger quantity for a much lower price. Dhgate can get you a smaller quantity that you can never get at Alibaba because Dhgates' minimum order quantities are lower and therefore you're going to pay a little more. But you can get also faster and free shipping almost every time.

Pro tip: it is really effective to start with your first supplier from here and then move over to a supplier from Alibaba or if you like the supplier here and they can give you a larger quantity for a lower price and be competitive, continue with such supplier.

Again, Dhgate is very safe compared to Alibaba. I'm not saying you can't get scammed, but it's much safer. Though you're going to pay more for it, you're going to get it faster and you don't need as much money. That's why Dhgate is a great place to start sourcing for a supplier. Be careful out there I'm sure if you follow the process above, it will be easier and better.

CHAPTER 3

HOW TO BRAND YOUR FBA BUSINESS

In this section, you will discover the top six tips for branding your product.

- **Choosing a name**

Use a service like https://www.namecheckr.com/ when you're choosing a name. Aside from checking for the availability of a domain name, it also automatically checks if the name is available on Facebook, Pinterest, and all other social media platforms. The best way to choose is to come up with a generic name that could be used for multiple products to cover for product expansions later. Make sure that you create all your social media accounts with the same name.

- **Get the domain.**

Once you've chosen your name, make sure that you buy the domain. Later you can use it to build an e-commerce shop. Use a service like godaddy.com.

- **Design a logo.**

You can use Upwork, 99designs or Fiverr to design a simple logo to go with your brand new name. Now for a $100 to $200, you can get multiple submissions and alterations until you create the absolute perfect logo for your brand.

- **Registered trademark.**

Register your brand name on https://www.uspto.gov/. You're going to need to prove that you are already using the brand, so Photoshop your logo onto your planned product and use a template to create an e-commerce store on your new domain. Add the product photo, the details, and the description to make sure it's live and that you have listed an item for sale. Then submit a screenshot of your product available for sale as evidence that you are already using the trademark.

- **Register with Amazon.**

Once you've registered the trademark, you can now go through the process of registering your brand on Amazon. This has so many additional benefits such as protecting your listing. Sometimes other sellers will see that you're selling well and they want to copy your product by selling fakes copied right off of your listing. If you've already registered the brand, you can ask Amazon to remove these fake sellers and as the brand owner, you get to decide who is allowed to sell your product.

- **Branding your product**

It's a lot of work to get a brand up and running. But once you do it, the e-commerce site is up; it's trademarked and registered on Amazon. Then, you can add it to your product directly. You can do this either on an insert card or the product packaging. Well branded products increase the value of an item substantially. The difference between the hundred-dollar T-shirt from a popular brand like Gucci, and a seven dollar t-shirt from Wal-Mart is just the branding.

CHAPTER 4

HOW TO SET UP YOUR AMAZON SELLER ACCOUNT

In this chapter, you will learn how to set up your Amazon seller account, and how feedback relates to sales. Let's get right into it.

If I had to narrow it down to five main steps to creating your Amazon seller account, they would be;

- **Step 1: Create** a new email address for this. Even if you're a buyer on Amazon you're using Amazon. So, create a whole new email address for your seller account, it's going to make things a lot easier for you.
- **Step 2:** On Amazon.com, go down to the bottom of the page and simply click on sell on Amazon. You have two choices here, either $0.99 per sale or $39.99 a month with a free trial.

Pro tip: I highly recommend you get the professional account at $39.99 a month because you have the free trial option to go along with it.

Step 3: Go ahead and click on start selling, accept the terms and conditions, and click "Continue." Put your address in here, your city or town, put your real number here. You'd need to put your credit card on file for billing when you choose the $39.99 a month option.

If you can put a different one than you usually use to purchase on Amazon, that'd be fantastic. Not compulsory, but if you can, it'd be perfect. Also, I think you can actually use a prepaid card here as well. So you would fill all that out. Click the 'save and continue' button.

- **Step 4: Input your real phone number here.**

You're going to click call me now or send me a text and they're going to call you, you're going to pick up the phone. By default, you're going to say hello but it's going to be Amazon. You're going to be given a little code after you choose the 'call me' option, a box is going to pop up on the screen, input the code in the box and voila, you're verified.

- **Step 5: Launch the interview wizard.**

Here, Amazon just wants some information about you for tax purposes, and they won't pay you until you fill that out. But you don't have to fill it out right away till you get up and running. Then, at any other time that is convenient for you and you see the word 'tax or interview wizard', take the time to complete this task. It'll only take a minute or two to fill it out and complete the set up of your account.

That's about everything it takes for you to open your Amazon seller account.

How to calculate your profit margins
In this section, you will discover how to calculate your profits. You do so by using a tool called the FBA calculator.

Google 'FBA calculator' without the quotes, then, open the first link on the search page. If you're an Amazon seller already or if you're thinking about selling on Amazon, this is a nice tool to be able to figure out exactly what you're going to be making on your potential product or your current products on Amazon.

Make sure the minimum price of the product you would like to sell is $20, otherwise, you won't be making any profit. The reason is that Amazon takes FBA fees for fulfilling and warehousing your product, so you're going to be out for at least four or five bucks for that, sometimes up to eight bucks so you want to keep that in mind

Here is a video that shows you how to use the FBA calculator:

\>\> https://www.youtube.com/watch?v=azsZJMcIoJY

If you're thinking about selling on Amazon I would definitely recommend that you use this calculator when you're doing your research.

How feedback relates to sales.

In this section, you'll discover...

- How it can affect your business in the future,
- And whether or not it's wise to solicit feedback from your buyers.

To start off, seller feedback is absolutely vital to any healthy Amazon business. It's a really great report card that buyers can use to determine who they want to spend their money with and who they can trust. Feedback is critical for one major reason... Trust.

Your buyers can look at your feedback and look at different comments to see if they want to trust you with their money. Having a great feedback score has an inherent advantage because you will capture more sales from those buyers that really take their time to research and look at the merchants that they're spending their money with.

But considering how things go on Amazon, your feedback score is going to have a completely different effect. Your feedback score is going to directly affect how often you receive the buy box; recent consumer studies show buyers are taking less and less time over the last few years to make a purchasing decision.

When they do look at a seller's feedback they are typically looking at five comments or fewer. Only about 73% of all consumers report that they are affected by things like feedback score. So they are making decisions much faster and this feeds right into the way that Amazon does business.

With the increase in purchases from mobile devices and with prime memberships, the Amazon consumer is not doing any research whatsoever most of the times. So, having the buy box is critical because so many people are doing the one-click methods of buying and that's really the biggest way that feedback will affect your business going into the future.

More buy box opportunities mean more sales. More sales mean more organic feedbacks and it becomes a cycle. What keeps this cycle running is the way that you run your business. The way that you run your business is going to make or break this entire pattern from the very beginning of your Amazon journey.

If you source for great products, describe them correctly, ship them with care and you provide excellent customer engagement, you are conducting your business in a way where the feedback is going to come and it's going to be positive generally.

Also because of your ability to engage your customer, when you do not get a positive feedback you will be in a better place to handle the situation right away. Handling those issues with great urgency really leaves an impression on buyers and often you can subtly get their help in removing negative feedback.

If you are a new seller on Amazon and you still have to just launch under your store name, these are the practices that are absolutely critical for you to adopt. The last thing that you want is to finally get your first feedback and have it not be a four or five; this will really put you in a bad place as far as feedback percentage is concerned.

Nobody likes to see a low feedback score and it's going to impair your ability to finally get the buy box. Once you are getting some feedbacks you should see a small uptick in sales as you do become 'buy box' eligible. So the question arises "if feedback is so critical, should I be contacting buyers and asking them to leave me feedback?"

Answer: This is going to be a very personal answer and what I would tell you is to be careful especially if you are new. If you are going to begin reaching out to your buyers asking for feedback, you really want to make sure of a couple of things.

First, your business has to absolutely be ready. You need to be extremely sure about your products, your methods, and your process. If you are still learning your way, you are bound to make more mistakes in the beginning than you realize (happened to me as well).

When you're new, I would advise you not to solicit feedback from your buyers unless you are absolutely sure you are getting it right all of the time. If you do solicit feedback from your buyers and there are holes in your process or there are things that you could be doing better, you could really be opening up a can of worms and sometimes the feedback that you're going to get may not be what you're actually expecting.

The second thing that I would say is that you look at feedback differently. You should look at feedback as your way of life because that is the voice of your buyer and a lot of times they will leave you some real golden nuggets in there about things that you may be able to change about your process that could really have a big impact on the way your buyer perceives your business.

Though it doesn't always happen, it can be really frustrating sometimes when you get a three or even sometimes a four and the comment that's left gives no clue about why it was not a perfect experience. Sometimes they could say that everything was great and the package arrived early and they'll still give you a four, sometimes they'll leave a "three" and they'll say they were happy!

I would absolutely chase a "three" because a neutral is the same as a negative. If it's not a positive, it takes away from your overall percentage. I would either reach out to the buyer if there was an issue or quite frankly if it doesn't look like there is anything that was your fault, if it's an FBA issue, I would immediately move for feedback removal.

The reason why I bring up the "three" issue is that in the case of a four, you get a positive feedback and it positively affects your feedback score, even though it's not a perfect five. Some of the raging debate is whether you would remove the four or not. Here's what I think; a four is a positive feedback if you're going to take points off of the board you should really have a great reason for it.

Either there is something detrimental in the comment that truly impacted the buyer's experience and took that five down to a four or something is said that reflects negatively on your business. Generally speaking, a four is going to help your feedback score but very slightly hurt your star rating. Does star rating matters? I would say yes and no if you have a star rating of a 4.0 or a 4.2, I would say you definitely need to focus on getting more fives.

But if your star rating is up at between 4.8 and 4.9, I would tell you not to ever take a four off of the board. With the number of buyers that are doing one-click purchases on Amazon prime, I would honestly tell you not to worry about it because most of them are going to add the item to the cart or pay for it without even seeing your star rating.

If you've got the buy box and they're going to purchase your item, it's not visible until they click through. So I would honestly say that you should not focus on your star rating because it doesn't have the same impact as your overall feedback percentage or when soliciting feedback from a buyer.

Imagine yourself in the shoes of the buyer and here is my own experience: as a buyer when I first make a purchase from Amazon, I receive an email which is an auto confirmation to let me know that the purchase has been made, then, typically I get a second email from Amazon letting me know that my item has been shipped.

What a lot of sellers don't know is that after the item is delivered, Amazon gives it a resting period of a couple of days and then Amazon sends me a reminder already asking me if I could leave a feedback. So that's already three emails and I'm not the kind of buyer that likes to receive emails - that's three emails just from Amazon. Now, let's say that you have a service that sends emails out for you to try to procure feedback.

By the time I've gotten those three emails from Amazon, I have either already left you feedback or I'm just a buyer that never leaves feedback. By the time you solicit feedback from me either manually or through an outside service, I'm already beginning to feel spammed.

If you are one of those sellers that has more than one email set to go out, by the time I get that second email from your service that's the fifth email that I have gotten on this purchase. At that point, I myself am probably going to get a little irritated and it could inspire a negative feedback. Whatever the case may be, I'm one of those buyers that you're completely wasting your money on with an outside service.

Keep it in mind that you always do run the risk of having the opposite effect that you think you're going to have by reaching out for feedback through outside services. This is a clear issue with soliciting feedback from all buyers; you never know what's going to come back to you.

You could be soliciting feedback that can negatively affect your account. Even if the feedback is removable you would have to go through the process of getting it removed. Also, keep in mind that a lot of sellers are reporting that Amazon lately has been a lot more hesitant to just remove feedback automatically so it can be a long process and it can be time-consuming for you.

In my opinion and I am speaking based on my experience, never chase feedback. I believe that if you run a really good business, handle your products really well, package them with care, you are incredibly communicative and responsive when a buyer does reach out to you, the feedback is going to come and when it does, it's going to be consistently a "five".

Also, I do not believe that it is necessary to employ an outside service for the purposes of generating feedback as it could have a negative impact on that buyers' overall experience.

CHAPTER 5

HOW TO AUTOMATE YOUR DROP SHIPPING ORDERS

Is there a way to automate your drop shipping orders?

Personally, I don't think there's any way you can do this fully automated, but an obvious answer is to outsource it. I'm not aware of any plug-in or software or integration between Amazon and Alibaba or Dhgate that allows you to do that on autopilot.

If you find it, let me know because I'm going to use it. But what I would suggest you do is to look for freelancers on sites like Upwork. In fact, I would just look on Upwork because you know you don't need any other site for that. Upwork is a great place to find freelancers and in your case, you want to find a virtual assistant.

You can create a job posting, and ideally, you want to look at applicants' reputation, work history and that way you can find great virtual assistants on Upwork.

Then, you can invite them for an interview once you've found a couple of good ones. Ideally, you would want to test each of them to know if they would be a good fit for you and your business.

I would recommend finding virtual assistants in the Philippines. I've worked with people in South America, India and in the Philippines. Personally, I think people in the Philippines are the most awesome virtual assistants and freelancers because they have a really good work ethic, they're really cheap, they have perfect English and they're pretty skilled.

So if I would compare Indian freelancers and people from the Philippines, I would probably recommend going with the Philippines, create a job posting on Upwork and then give them instructions. Tell them exactly what to do. I wouldn't pay more than $3 per hour for a good virtual assistant in the Philippines.

So it's really cheap on your side. So all you have to do is focus on the marketing and on the selling (preferably, Facebook Ads), and adding new products to your store.

If you don't want to outsource it to freelancers, you can make use of outsourcing companies.

Ordoro is one the most reliable outsourcing companies you can make use of. Check them out at https://www.ordoro.com/

CHAPTER 6

THE TOP 5 BEST SELLING NICHES

Here are the top 5 categories I'm going to give you...

5. Sporting Goods.

They're commonly used all over the world. Certainly in the United States when it comes to e-commerce, it has actually exploded - it's been booming. To get ideas, you can look at TV programs like the softball knees or the baseball knee show.

Its accessories really are a good one because the competition isn't that stiff compared to sports gadgets. When we're talking electronics, you're not going to actually get into making computers because Apple's got that market cornered.

You're not going to get into making flat-screen TVs. But there are a million TV and computer accessories that you can sell. Analyzing the sports market now, there are literally hundreds of sports if you really think about it. From martial arts to rollerblade; the sporting goods niche is an amazing niche.

4. Hardware and tools

I've worked with a lot of clients who've done really well in these niches because they're things that people need on a daily basis. Again, I'm not saying you should compete directly with Walmart, but there are so many different accessories - bits, hinges, hoses, fittings, right mirrors, RV accessories and similar hardware and tools are examples of these accessories. So, it's those kinds of necessities that people need. So, the hardware and tools niche comes in at a strong number four.

3. Organizational products

This is where people get stuck, they start out really small. There is an unlimited amount of organizational products that you can actually sell your e-commerce store. Don't get stuck on drawer organizers and closet organizers, there's so much other stuff.

2. Creative storage

Creative storage is hot right now. It's definitely something you should look into. The biggest reasons for this are that it's evergreen and it's one of those things that you can sell all year-round. With creative storage, it really digs deep. One of those products that are making waves right now is pet and baby related storage products.

Let me tell you something about the people who buy in the parent-baby market; I got four kids and a lot of you guys out there have babies and pets and guess what you spare no expense. That's the biggest thing with this market - people literally spare no expense. Also, these are markets that evolve all the time. Now, I don't know lots of pet designs for kids but these are some awesome stuff.

For example, I have the black lab dog that I've always wanted; it would be the most spoiled dog because I would find the coolest oven. So these are the niches/sub-niches that I highly recommend. But ideally, you do a lot of research on each of them because each of them goes a lot deeper than we've covered and product research is something that you should always keep in your mind. It is super important. Through it, you can as well do all your comparisons, your back-channeling, and all your reviews.

Make sure you've really set up the basics to make sure there's a good market. But there are lots of good markets and with some minimal marketing efforts in setting these things up, you got a good chance.

1. Alternative energy based products

It's a niche that I've been dabbling into but with moderate success. There are really not many dominant players in this niche. If you have any gadget, one of the biggest weak points of any gadget is batteries; they are always weak and it doesn't matter whether your gadget is an iPhone, a galaxy or those electric skateboards.

This niche is the number one product based niche that people haven't really dominated. Another obvious product that can be sold in this niche is solar chargers.

But there are so many iterations and if you look through these different manufacturer/supplier sites, talk to these manufacturers and get just a little bit creative, you could strike a gold mine. You would want to think about where things are going in the future because on the big scale you can only compete so far with certain things.

In my opinion, that's where things are going. Batteries are at their peak, Elon Musk and Tesla built the biggest battery plant but we keep hitting this peak. So, based on being able to charge, the resources of charge and the things that could be charged, you can create and sell products based on all these.

While you use them, what about getting smarter. For example, think about a Logitech keyboard that's actually solar based and one that never dies. I've had one for a few years and it's just unstoppable. It's the best keyboard and it's based on the same principle I'm talking about – getting a little bit creative.

Utilize this principle and put it in other product. My advice is to really get creative with your products and think outside the box because no software can help you to see that. My goal is not just to make you five bucks right now; rather it is to make you a real business that could grow into an asset in the future.

So, that's my point of view on the top niches that you could utilize to make a full-time income on Amazon. You can utilize these niches on Shopify or whatever other platforms you happen to sell. Figure out what you're going to do in your business, take a solid niche and put in the work every day.

The most important thing is to actually take action on a daily basis if you don't do that you got no shot. Never give up, work extremely hard and believe in yourself. No one's going to believe in you if you don't believe in yourself. The best thing I ever did was to believe in myself. I know it sounds all 'Tony Robbins' ish, but it's true I had nothing going on but I believed in myself.

I put in hard work it all came together nicely for me. Look, I'm not a trillionaire, I just worked really hard and have a lot of fun. That's the thing - find something you love to do, do it and just have a lot of fun.

CONCLUSION

You just learned how to get started and succeed with drop shipping using Amazon FBA. And that means you can now start your drop shipping business with confidence that you will succeed. To that end, let's quickly recap what you learned over the last six chapters:

- You learned the best ways to pick a profitable product to sell.
- You found out how to effectively work with overseas suppliers.
- Plus you ever discovered a slick way to the top 5 best selling niches.

Give yourself a pat on the back, because you're now all set to succeed with drop shipping using Amazon FBA!

If You Like My Book Please Write A Review On Amazon?

www.ingramcontent.com/pod-product-compliance
Lightning Source LLC
Chambersburg PA
CBHW050024230526
45470CB00003B/1119